Teach & Learn
Microsoft Visual Basic
with 26
Hands-on Projects

MOHAMMAD J. MOROVATI

CONTENTS

ACKNOWLEDGMENTS

Special thanks to **Cecil Champenois** for the book revision.

Preface

Programming skill in any programming language is firstly related to the concept of algorithms and the art of problem comprehension and problem solving, secondly, mastering the features and tools of programming language to implement a solution strategy through continuous practice. In addition, patience, logical thinking, creativity, interest in teamwork, and a programmer are required.

In relation to learning and mastering the concepts of programming and programming language features and tools, maybe one of the best methods is to implement practical examples, applications, debugging them, changing them in various sectors, and ultimately, to propose ideas to develop projects. The book with the same approach implements and analyses 26 simple, practical, and commercial programming projects with the Visual Basic programming language as a typical educational programming language. In each project, the educational concepts of algorithms and Visual Basic features have been described as the educational goals of the project. Then, a summary of the design, implementation, and execution process of the project has been reviewed. In the end, the author proposes developing ideas to help readers develop the project. In each project, the project GUI image and the source code of the project are given.

Many of the projects discussed in the book are simple forms of commercial and industrial projects. Projects presented by the author are designed to cover many Visual Basic programming and algorithm concepts.

At the beginning of the book, a summary of the educational objectives of the projects is discussed. At the end of the book, Visual Basic programming language commands and function references are included.

The author recommends that readers conduct researches on data structures, design tips, and speed of algorithms, while trying to develop projects.

1

Project files are available at :

Https://sites.google.com/site/itbooklets/VB

LEARNING OBJECTIVES

Book readers will be familiar with the following items through studying and implementation of the projects discussed in the book and development of the project with the author's ideas:

- Understanding and using different types of data and variables in Visual Basic
- Understanding and using arithmetic, comparison, and logical expressions
- Understanding and using IF ELSE and Select Case conditional structures
- **Understanding and using** basic Visual Basic functions such as InputBox and MsgBox and Visual Basic controls such as Form, Checkbox, TextBox, Label, PictureBox, Command button, Frame, Option button, and setting their properties
- Understanding and using global variables in programs
- Understanding the concept of security in authentication to systems and applications
- Understanding and using programs with multiple active and passive forms and connecting the forms
- Understanding and using the functions of system date and system clock (time) in Visual Basic
- **Introduction to session expire concept** (Session Timeout) in system security
- Understanding and using the timer control for timing implementation in Visual Basic
- Understanding the concept of Input Field Validation in electronic

forms
- **Understanding and using** Pattern Matching Characters in strings and words evaluation
- Understanding and using string functions and operators such as Like
- Understanding and using mathematical and trigonometric functions in Visual Basic
- **Understanding** the function of generating random numbers and using them in Visual Basic
- Understanding and using date functions in Visual Basic including ISDATE, CDATE, DateDiff, and their parameters
- Learning how to design and use time counters in Visual Basic
- Understanding and using For... Next loop structure in applications
- Understanding and using the functions of read and write data in files (File Operations) in Visual Basic
- **Understanding and using control** arrays and its navigation in Visual Basic
- Understanding and using the functions of operating system clipboard operations
- Understanding and using ListBox and ComboBox controls in Visual Basic
- Understanding and using the mouse and keyboard events and functions and their arguments in Visual Basic
- Understanding the concept of Shortcut key in programs
- Understanding the definition and structure of arrays and their application in Visual Basic
- Understanding and using Bubble Sort data sorting algorithm
- Understanding and using Linear and Binary data search algorithms
- Understanding Do... Loop, loop structure used for indefinite repetition, and its application
- Understanding and using the Scroll control in Visual Basic
- Understanding and using the RGB color function to define RGB color in Visual Basic
- **Understanding and using** DirListBox, FileListBox, and DriveListBox **controls** for system file management.
- Understanding and using functions and commands to manage files and directories in Visual Basic
- Understanding the concepts of object-oriented programming and implementing it in Visual Basic
- Understanding the structure of a Text Editor and designing it
- Understanding and using the Common Dialog control to create common dialog boxes, such as opening files, saving files, printing

files, and setting the font and color of the text files

- Understanding and using the menu design tool for GUI applications in Visual Basic
- Introduction to the subroutine call in Visual Basic
- Understanding how the Visual basic application and Microsoft Office software are linked to each other
- Understanding and using the Word object properties and methods for working with Microsoft Word text files
- Understanding and using Windows API routines stored in DLL files
- Understanding the API Viewer utility to view and call API routines with the Declare statement in Visual Basic
- Understanding and using the functions for managing running processes in the operating system
- Understanding the structure of Multimedia Player software
- Understanding the "MultiMedia Control" component in Visual Basic to play audio and video files
- Understanding and using properties and procedures of the "MultiMedia Control" component such as Play, Pause, Stop, Next, Seek, etc.

Project 1: The energy consumption cost calculation based on the stepped consumption pattern

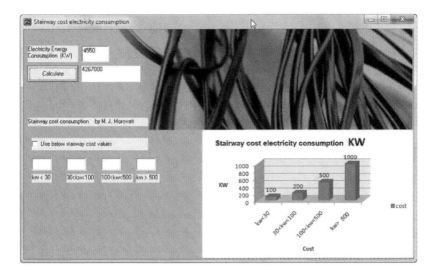

Educational goals of the project:

Understanding the conditional structures in algorithms (here, Select Case structure)

Understanding and using CheckBox, TextBox, Label, PictureBox and Command button controls in Visual Basic

Summary of design, implementation, and execution of the project:

The program receives the amount of consumed energy in KW, and then energy cost is   calculated based on the default stepped cost pattern or operator stepped cost pattern.

Development proposals:

Information of consumer unit and consumption period is received, and the cost is calculated based on the information. Final information is saved in a file as a bill.

Project source code:

```
Private Sub Check1_Click()
If (Check1.Value = vbChecked) Then
    Text2.Enabled = True
    Text3.Enabled = True
    Text4.Enabled = True
    Text5.Enabled = True
ElseIf (Check1.Value = vbUnchecked) Then
    Text2.Enabled = False
    Text3.Enabled = False
    Text4.Enabled = False
    Text5.Enabled = False
End If

End Sub

Private Sub Command1_Click()
Dim intKW As Integer
Dim lngCost As Long

If (Check1.Value = vbUnchecked) Then

    step1 = 100
    step2 = 200
    step3 = 500
    step4 = 1000

    intKW = Val(Text1.Text)
    Select Case intKW
    Case Is <= 30
    lngCost = intKW * step1
    Case Is <= 100
```

```
    lngCost = 30 * step1 + (intKW - 30) * step2
  Case Is <= 500
    lngCost = 30 * step1 + 70 * step2 + (intKW - 100) * step3
  Case Else
    lngCost = 30 * step1 + 70 * step2 + 400 * step3 + (intKW - 500) *
step4
  End Select
  Label2.Caption = lngCost

ElseIf (Check1.Value = vbChecked) Then
  step1 = Val(Text2.Text)
  step2 = Val(Text3.Text)
  step3 = Val(Text4.Text)
  step4 = Val(Text5.Text)

  intKW = Val(Text1.Text)
  Select Case intKW
  Case Is <= 30
  lngCost = intKW * step1
  Case Is <= 100
    lngCost = 30 * step1 + (intKW - 30) * step2
  Case Is <= 500
    lngCost = 30 * step1 + 70 * step2 + (intKW - 100) * step3
  Case Else
    lngCost = 30 * step1 + 70 * step2 + 400 * step3 + (intKW - 500) *
step4
  End Select
  Label2.Caption = lngCost

End If

End Sub

Private Sub Form_Load()
Text2.Enabled = False
Text3.Enabled = False
Text4.Enabled = False
Text5.Enabled = False
Check1.Value = vbUnchecked
End Sub
```

Project 2: E-shopping and total price calculation

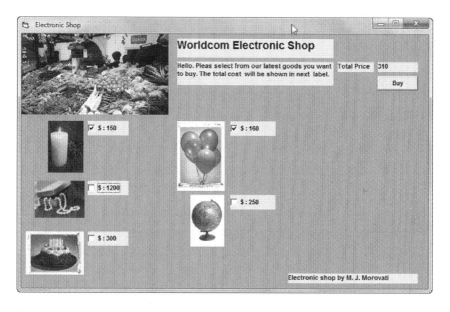

Educational goals of the project:

Understanding and using global variables and Checkbox control in Visual Basic

Summary of design, implementation, and execution of the project:

The user selects or deselects goods, and then the program calculates the total price of the user basket using "LngPrice" global variable.

Development proposals:

Goods are classified into different topics and pages. Personal information and users' e-mail are received, and the users orders are composed and saved in a file.

Project source code:

```
Dim lngPrice As Long


Private Sub Check1_Click()

If (Check1.Value = vbChecked) Then
    lngPrice = lngPrice + 150
ElseIf (Check1.Value = vbUnchecked) Then
    lngPrice = lngPrice - 150
End If
Label3.Caption = lngPrice

End Sub

Private Sub Check2_Click()

If (Check2.Value = vbChecked) Then
    lngPrice = lngPrice + 1200
ElseIf (Check2.Value = vbUnchecked) Then
    lngPrice = lngPrice - 1200
End If
Label3.Caption = lngPrice

End Sub

Private Sub Check3_Click()

If (Check3.Value = vbChecked) Then
    lngPrice = lngPrice + 300
ElseIf (Check3.Value = vbUnchecked) Then
    lngPrice = lngPrice - 300
End If
Label3.Caption = lngPrice

End Sub
```

```vb
Private Sub Check4_Click()

If (Check4.Value = vbChecked) Then
    lngPrice = lngPrice + 160
ElseIf (Check4.Value = vbUnchecked) Then
    lngPrice = lngPrice - 160
End If
Label3.Caption = lngPrice

End Sub

Private Sub Check5_Click()

If (Check5.Value = vbChecked) Then
    lngPrice = lngPrice + 250
ElseIf (Check5.Value = vbUnchecked) Then
    lngPrice = lngPrice - 250
End If
Label3.Caption = lngPrice

End Sub

Private Sub Command1_Click()
InputBox ("Enter your name, address and contact informations.")
End Sub

Private Sub Form_Load()
lngPrice = 0
Label3.Caption = lngPrice
End Sub
```

Project 3: Electronic test and test score calculation

Educational goals of the project:

Understanding and using frame and Option button control in Visual Basic

Understanding visible and invisible properties of controls in Visual Basic

Summary of design, implementation, and execution of the project:

By placing frame control in the form according to number of test questions, it is possible to place and group option buttons as choices of questions in the form. According to the characteristics of the option button control, users can choose only one choice among question choices. By the end of the test, the test is corrected, and the score is calculated and displayed while test questions become invisible.

Development proposals:

Put more questions in multiple forms and consider a page as test correction info and answers. Test results are saved in a file.

Project source code

```
Dim mark As Byte

Private Sub Command1_Click()
Text3.Text = Text1.Text

Text2.Text = mark * 20 / 3
If (mark * 20 / 3 >= 10) Then
    Text2.BackColor = vbGreen
Else
    Text2.BackColor = vbRed
End If

Frame1.Visible = False
Frame2.Visible = False
Frame3.Visible = False

End Sub

Private Sub Form_Load()
mark = 0
Option1.Value = 0
Option2.Value = 0
Option3.Value = 0
Option4.Value = 0
Option5.Value = 0
```

```
Option6.Value = 0
Option7.Value = 0
Option8.Value = 0
Option9.Value = 0
Option10.Value = 0
Option11.Value = 0
Option12.Value = 0
End Sub

Private Sub Option11_Click()
mark = mark + 1
End Sub

Private Sub Option3_Click()
mark = mark + 1
End Sub

Private Sub Option8_Click()
mark = mark + 1

End Sub
```

Project 4: User authentication in security system with restricted number of login attempts

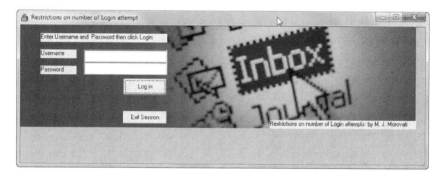

Educational goals of the project:

Understanding the concept of security in authentication to systems and applications

Understanding programs with multiple active and passive forms and connecting the forms

Summary of design, implementation, and execution of the project:

The program uses two TextBox controls to receive username and password from the user to authenticate the user in the system. Global variable, "attempt", counts the number of login buttons pressed. If "attempt" variable reaches specified limitation (here, 5 attempts limitation), the login button is disabled. If authenticated, the main form of application is activated. Username and password are set "bm861249" and "62634642".

Development proposals:

The data entered in failed attempts are saved in a history log file for security analyses. Design registration form for new users and add new users to a transportable file.

Project source code:

```
Dim attempt As Byte

Private Sub Command1_Click()

Dim username As String
Dim password As String

username = Text1.Text
password = Text2.Text

If (username = "bm861249") And (password = "62634642") Then
    Form1.Hide
    Form2.Show
Else
    attempt = attempt + 1
End If

If (attempt = 5) Then
    Command1.Enabled = False
    Command1.Caption = "Login failed!"
End If
End Sub

Private Sub Command2_Click()
End
End Sub

Private Sub Form_Load()
Form2.Hide
End Sub
```

Project 5: User authentication in security system with restricted login date and time

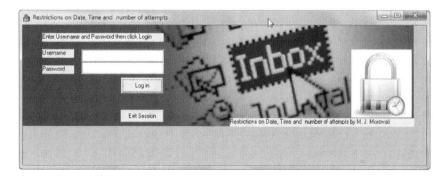

Educational goals of the project:

Understanding the concept of security in authentication to systems and applications

Understanding and using logical and comparison operators, and its composition

Understanding the system date (Date) and system time (Time) functions in Visual Basic

Summary of design, implementation, and execution of the project:

A new restriction is added to the previous project, more than a restriction in a number of attempts; restriction on date and time of login, using the Date and Time functions and IF ELSE conditional structure. Here, time and date restrictions are determined on 1.1.2012 to 01.01.2016 and 1pm to 10pm.

Development proposals:

The data entered in failed attempts are saved in a history log file for security analyses. Design registration form for new users. For each user, according to the time, he is allowed to enter and use the system; date and time restrictions are set separately.

Project source code:

```
Dim attempt As Byte
Dim TimeInit As Date
Dim DateInit As Date

Private Sub Command1_Click()

Dim username As String
Dim password As String

username = Text1.Text
password = Text2.Text

If (username = "bm861249") And (password = "62634642") Then
    Form1.Hide
    Form2.Show
Else
    attempt = attempt + 1
End If

If (attempt = 5) Then
    Command1.Enabled = False
    Command1.Caption = "Login failed!"
End If
End Sub

Private Sub Command2_Click()
End
End Sub

Private Sub Form_Load()
```

```
TimeInit = Time()
DateInit = Date
If Not (DateInit > #1/1/2012# And DateInit < #1/1/2016#) Then
   int1 = MsgBox("Access Denied For Date restriction, 1/1/2012 to
1/1/2016 ", vbOK + vbCritical, "Access Denied")
   End
End If

If Not (TimeInit > #1:00:00 PM# And TimeInit < #10:00:00 PM#) Then
   int1 = MsgBox("Access Denied For Time restriction, 1:00:00 PM to
7:00:00 PM ", vbOK + vbCritical, "Access Denied")
   End
End If

Form2.Hide
End Sub
```

Project 6: User authentication in a security system with login time limit

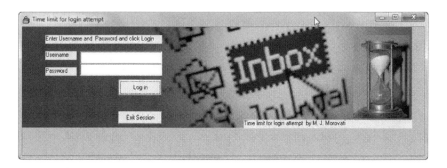

Educational goals of the project:

Understanding the concept of security in authentication to systems and applications

Introduction to session expire concept (Session Timeout) in system security

Understanding and using Timer control in Visual Basic

Summary of design, implementation, and execution of the project:

Using the Timer control and setting it, it is possible for a specified event to occur in specified time. Here, a 60-second delay occurs and as the user attempts to login, the Login button becomes disabled and a "Session timeout" message is displayed.

Development proposals:

The data entered in failed attempts and the data entered in expired sessions are saved in an event log for future security analyses.

Project source code:

```vb
Dim attempt As Byte
Dim TimeLimit As Integer


Private Sub Command1_Click()

Dim username As String
Dim password As String

If (Val(TimeLimit) > 60) Then
    Command1.Enabled = False
    Command1.Caption = "Login failed! Session timeout"
    Exit Sub
End If

username = Text1.Text
password = Text2.Text
If (username = "bm861249") And (password = "62634642") Then
    Form1.Hide
    Form2.Show
Else
    attempt = attempt + 1
End If

If (attempt = 5) Then
    Command1.Enabled = False
    Command1.Caption = "Login failed!"
End If
End Sub

Private Sub Command2_Click()
End
End Sub

Private Sub Form_Load()
```

```
Form2.Hide
End Sub

Private Sub Timer1_Timer()
TimeLimit = TimeLimit + 1
End Sub
```

Project 7: E-form with input data verification (E-form field validation)

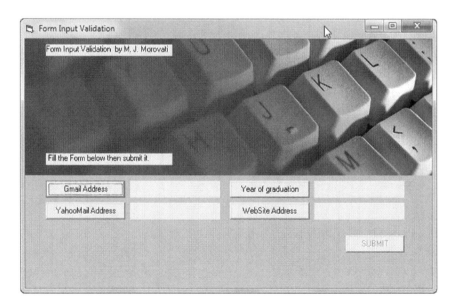

Educational goals of the project:

Understanding the concept of Input Field Validation

Understanding and using pattern matching characters and "Like" operation for comparing strings in Visual Basic

Understanding and using the indefinite Do... Loop, loop structure

Summary of design, implementation, and execution of the

project:

The program verifies input data with the pattern matching characters such as *, #,? using "Like" operator. For example, for a web page address, "www. *. *" is concerned. Using indefinite "Do... Loop" loop structure, asking the user to get the valid input data continues. Using "flag" variables, if all input data are valid, the submit button used for saving information becomes activated.

Development proposals:

Provide a message box so that in any error in user input data provides the user with correct form of the input data. Save data in a file after verifying it.

Project source code:

```
Dim str5 As String
Dim str6 As String
Dim year As Integer
Dim str8 As String


Dim flag1 As Byte
Dim flag2 As Byte
Dim flag3 As Byte
Dim flag4 As Byte




Private Sub Command1_Click()
MsgBox ("Your information :" & vbNewLine & str1 & vbNewLine & str2
& vbNewLine & str3 & vbNewLine & str4 & vbNewLine & str5 &
vbNewLine & str6 & vbNewLine & year & vbNewLine & str8 &
vbNewLine & vbNewLine & "Do you confirme it?")


End Sub
```

```
Private Sub Command6_Click()

Do
   str5 = InputBox("Enter Your Gmail Address :")
Loop While (str5 Like "*@gmail.com") = False

Label7.Caption = str5
Label7.BackColor = vbGreen

flag1 = 1
If ((flag1 + flag2 + flag3 + flag4) = 4) Then
   Command1.Enabled = True
End If
End Sub

Private Sub Command7_Click()


Do
   str6 = InputBox("Enter Your Yahoo Mail Address :")
Loop While (str6 Like "*@yahoo.com") = False

Label8.Caption = str6
Label8.BackColor = vbGreen

flag2 = 1
If ((flag1 + flag2 + flag3 + flag4) = 4) Then
   Command1.Enabled = True
End If
End Sub

Private Sub Command8_Click()


Do
   year = InputBox("Enter Your Year of graduation :")
Loop While (1900 < year And year < 2015) = False

Label9.Caption = year
Label9.BackColor = vbGreen

flag3 = 1
If ((flag1 + flag2 + flag3 + flag4) = 4) Then
```

```
    Command1.Enabled = True
End If
End Sub

Private Sub Command9_Click()


Do
    str8 = InputBox("Enter Your Website Address:")
Loop While (str8 Like "www.*.*") = False

Label10.Caption = str8
Label10.BackColor = vbGreen

flag4 = 1
If ((flag1 + flag2 + flag3 + flag4) = 4) Then
    Command1.Enabled = True
End If
End Sub

Private Sub Form_Load()
Command1.Enabled = False

End Sub
```

Project 8: Math and trigonometric function calculator program

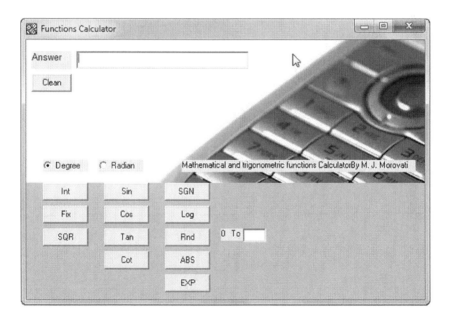

Educational goals of the project:

Understanding and using mathematical and trigonometric functions in Visual Basic

Summary of design, implementation, and execution of the project:

After receiving the input data, according to the selected function and adjust degrees or radians, the function code is applied to the input data. Functions include INT, FIX, SQR (square root), SIN (sinus), COS (cosine), TAN (tangent), COT (cotangent), SGN, LOG (logarithm), RND (random number generation), ABS (absolute), and EXP (e ^ input number).

Development proposals:

Add some additional functions like Sinh (x) and Arcsin (x) to the program.

Separate calculator program into simple and engineering states. Add four main operations (+ - * /) to the program to eventually become similar to the Windows operating system calculator.

Project source code:

```
Dim dbN As Double

Private Sub Command1_Click()
Text1.Text = Int(Val(Text1.Text))

End Sub

Private Sub Command10_Click()

Dim intN As Integer
intN = Val(Text2.Text)
Text1.Text = Int(intN * Rnd())
Text2.Text = ""

End Sub

Private Sub Command11_Click()
Text1.Text = 0
End Sub

Private Sub Command12_Click()
dbN = Val(Text1.Text)
Text1.Text = Abs(dbN)
End Sub

Private Sub Command13_Click()
dbN = Val(Text1.Text)
```

```
Text1.Text = Exp(dbN)
End Sub

Private Sub Command2_Click()
Text1.Text = Fix(Val(Text1.Text))

End Sub

Private Sub Command3_Click()
dbN = Val(Text1.Text)
Text1.Text = Sqr(dbN)

End Sub

Private Sub Command4_Click()
dbN = Val(Text1.Text)
If (Option1.Value = True) Then
    Text1.Text = Sin(dbN * 3.1415 / 180)
ElseIf (Option2.Value = True) Then
    Text1.Text = Sin(dbN)
End If

End Sub

Private Sub Command5_Click()
dbN = Val(Text1.Text)
If (Option1.Value = True) Then
    Text1.Text = Cos(dbN * 3.1415 / 180)
ElseIf (Option2.Value = True) Then
    Text1.Text = Cos(dbN)
End If
End Sub

Private Sub Command6_Click()
dbN = Val(Text1.Text)
If (Option1.Value = True) Then
    Text1.Text = Tan(dbN * 3.1415 / 180)
ElseIf (Option2.Value = True) Then
    Text1.Text = Tan(dbN)
End If
End Sub

Private Sub Command7_Click()
```

```
dbN = Val(Text1.Text)
If (Option1.Value = True) Then
    Text1.Text = 1 / Tan(dbN * 3.1415 / 180)
ElseIf (Option2.Value = True) Then
    Text1.Text = 1 / Tan(dbN)
End If
End Sub

Private Sub Command8_Click()
dbN = Val(Text1.Text)
Text1.Text = Sgn(dbN)

End Sub

Private Sub Command9_Click()
dbN = Val(Text1.Text)
Text1.Text = Log(dbN)

End Sub

Private Sub Form_Load()
Option1.Value = True

End Sub
```

Project 9: A program to display the exact age in years, months, weeks, days, hours, minutes, and seconds with real-time updates

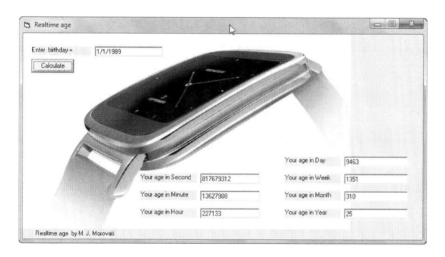

Educational goals of the project:

Understanding date-related functions in Visual Basic,including ISDATE, CDATE and DateDiff

Understanding and using Timer control in Visual Basic

Summary of design, implementation, and execution of the project:

The application receives Date of Birth and corrects its format with CDATE and ISDATE functions, and then applies the DateDiff function with its arguments (years, months, days, etc.) and displays the calculated values. The application uses a 1-second timer to update values constantly.

Project source code:

```
Dim bdate As Date
Private Sub Command1_Click()

If IsDate(Text1.Text) Then
   bdate = CDate(Text1.Text)
Else
   MsgBox "Invalid date!"
End If

Timer1.Enabled = True


End Sub

Private Sub Form_Load()
Timer1.Enabled = False

End Sub

Private Sub Timer1_Timer()

Dim sec As Long
Dim min As Long
Dim hour As Long
Dim day As Long
Dim week As Long
Dim month As Long
Dim year As Long

sec = DateDiff("s", bdate, Now)
min = DateDiff("n", bdate, Now)
hour = DateDiff("h", bdate, Now)
day = DateDiff("d", bdate, Now)
week = DateDiff("w", bdate, Now)
month = DateDiff("m", bdate, Now)
year = DateDiff("yyyy", bdate, Now)
```

```
Text2.Text = sec
Text3.Text = min
Text4.Text = hour
Text5.Text = day
Text6.Text = week
Text7.Text = month
Text8.Text = year

End Sub
```

Project 10: Time/cost management of computer users in internet cafes

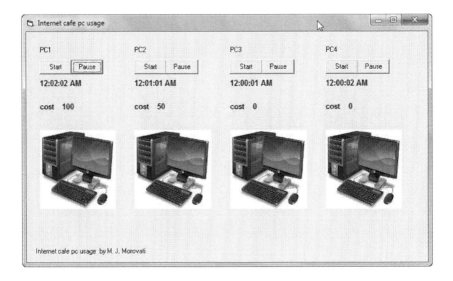

Educational goals of the project:
Understanding and using Timer control in Visual Basic

Summary of design, implementation, and execution of the project:

The application administers a computer user fee in an internet cafe with four computers. When a user uses a computer, application operator presses the Start button to activate the user timer. The timer starts counting upward from 12:00:00. Pressing the "pause" button will pause the timer, and the cost will be calculated and displayed using the DateDiff function. By pressing the "Pause" button again, the timer counting continues, and by pressing the "Start" button again, the timer restarts counting upward.

Development proposals:

The application receives computer user data and saves it with a user fee in a file. The cost of using the computers is calculated according to the application operator decision. The application considers two status sensors for each computer that checks local network connectivity and Internet connectivity and provide a monitoring tool for the café operator.

Project source code:

```
Dim i1 As Date
Dim i2 As Date
Dim i3 As Date
Dim i4 As Date

Private Sub Command1_Click()
i1 = 0
Timer1.Enabled = True
End Sub

Private Sub Command2_Click()
Timer1.Enabled = Not (Timer1.Enabled)
Label10.Caption = 50 * DateDiff("n", 0, i1)
End Sub

Private Sub Command3_Click()
i2 = 0
Timer2.Enabled = True
End Sub

Private Sub Command4_Click()
Timer2.Enabled = Not (Timer2.Enabled)
Label11.Caption = 50 * DateDiff("n", 0, i2)
End Sub

Private Sub Command5_Click()
```

```
i3 = 0
Timer3.Enabled = True
End Sub

Private Sub Command6_Click()
Timer3.Enabled = Not (Timer3.Enabled)
Label12.Caption = 50 * DateDiff("n", 0, i3)
End Sub

Private Sub Command7_Click()
i4 = 0
Timer4.Enabled = True
End Sub

Private Sub Command8_Click()
Timer4.Enabled = Not (Timer4.Enabled)
Label13.Caption = 50 * DateDiff("n", 0, i4)
End Sub

Private Sub Form_Load()

Timer1.Enabled = False
Timer2.Enabled = False
Timer3.Enabled = False
Timer4.Enabled = False
End Sub

Private Sub Timer1_Timer()
i1 = DateAdd("s", 1, i1)
Label1.Caption = i1
End Sub

Private Sub Timer2_Timer()
i2 = DateAdd("s", 1, i2)
Label2.Caption = i2
End Sub

Private Sub Timer3_Timer()
i3 = DateAdd("s", 1, i3)
Label3.Caption = i3
End Sub

Private Sub Timer4_Timer()
```

```
i4 = DateAdd("s", 1, i4)
Label4.Caption = i4
End Sub
```

Project 11: Consecutive number serie-generator with a file output

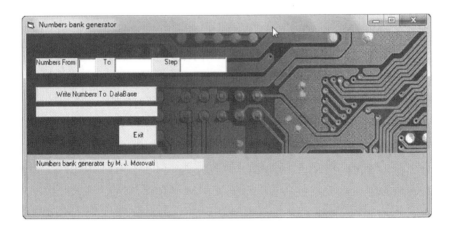

Educational goals of the project:

Understanding the concept of data sets and its application

Understanding and using For... Next loop structure

Understanding and using the functions of read and write data in files (File operations) in Visual Basic

Summary of design, implementation, and execution of the project:

Data sets are frequently used as input for various projects. This application uses a For... Next loop structure to generate a series of consecutive numbers. Loop parameters including start, end, and step, are received from the application user. Finally, numbers will be written in a file, and the "database is ready" message is displayed.

Development proposals:

The new application is capable of generating numbers, strings, and words with distinct patterns, such as cell phone number pattern, email address format, or password format.

Project source code:

```
Private Sub Command1_Click()
Label3.Caption = ""

Dim LngStart As Long
Dim LngEnd As Long
Dim IntStep As Integer
Dim DataBase As String
Dim i As Long


LngStart = Val(Text1.Text)
LngEnd = Val(Text2.Text)
IntStep = Val(Text3.Text)


DataBase = "DataBase.txt"
Open DataBase$ For Output As #1

For i = LngStart To LngEnd Step IntStep
    Print #1, i

Next i
Close #1

Label3.Caption = "DataBase is Ready ..."


End Sub

Private Sub Command2_Click()
```

```
End
End Sub

Private Sub Form_Load()
Label3.Caption = ""

End Sub
```

Project 12: Step by step Installation wizard of a software

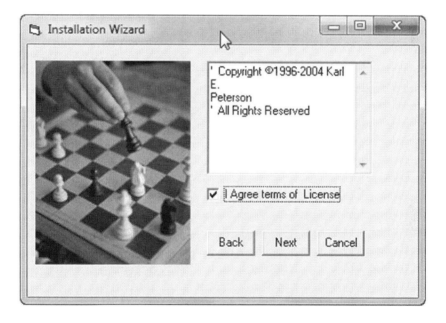

Educational goals of the project:

Understanding the software installation wizards

Understanding and using programs with multiple active and passive forms and connecting the forms

Summary of design, implementation, and execution of the project:

A software installation wizard is simulated (a chess computer game).

Pressing the "next" button in any form, the current form becomes hidden (Form.hide), and the next form in the wizard becomes activated (Form.show). Pressing the "back" button does it in reverse.

Development proposals:

In the installation wizard, the user is asked to specify a path to install the game, and a chess game file is copied in that path. A shortcut of the chess game file is created on the desktop.

Project source code:

```
Form 1
Private Sub Command2_Click()
Form1.Hide
Form2.Show
End Sub

Private Sub Command3_Click()
End
End Sub

Private Sub Form_Load()
Command1.Enabled = False

End Sub

Form 2
Private Sub Check1_Click()
If Check1.Value = vbChecked Then
   Command2.Enabled = True
Else
   Command2.Enabled = False
End If

End Sub

Private Sub Command1_Click()
Form2.Hide
Form1.Show
End Sub
```

```
Private Sub Command2_Click()
Form2.Hide
Form3.Show
End Sub

Private Sub Command3_Click()
End
End Sub

Private Sub Form_Load()
Command2.Enabled = False

End Sub

Form 3
Private Sub Command1_Click()
Form3.Hide
Form2.Show

End Sub

Private Sub Command3_Click()
End
End Sub

Private Sub Form_Load()
Command2.Enabled = False

End Sub
```

Project 13: Slideshow of images saved in gallery

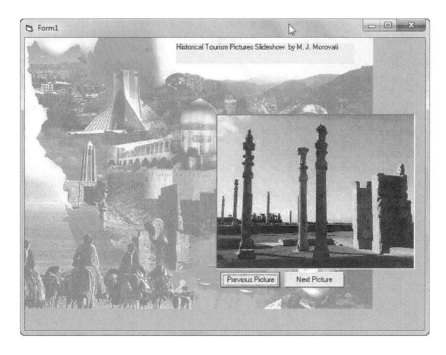

Educational goals of the project:

Understanding and using control arrays and its navigation in Visual Basic

Summary of design, implementation, and execution of the project:

At application runtime, a control array of "image control" (Image1) is created, and the images in the "shz" folder in the project directory are loaded into a control array (here, nine images of a historical place in the city of Shiraz).

With the "Next" and "Previous" buttons, current control (current image) becomes invisible, and the image after or before becomes visible. If you reach the last image, with the "Next" button, the image of the first image control will be visible, and if you reach the first image, with the "Previous" button, the image of the last image control will be visible.

Development proposals:

Include images of other places and cities in the project, and the user chooses a favorite place to see images of that place.

Project source code:

```
Dim counter As Byte

Private Sub Command1_Click()
Image1(counter).Visible = False

If (counter < 9) Then
    counter = counter + 1
Else
    counter = 1
End If
Image1(counter).Visible = True


End Sub

Private Sub Command2_Click()
Image1(counter).Visible = False

If (counter > 1) Then
    counter = counter - 1
Else
    counter = 9
End If
Image1(counter).Visible = True
End Sub
```

```
Private Sub Form_Load()
Load Image1(1)
Load Image1(2)
Load Image1(3)
Load Image1(4)
Load Image1(5)
Load Image1(6)
Load Image1(7)
Load Image1(8)
Load Image1(9)

Image1(1).Picture = LoadPicture("shz\im1.JPG")
Image1(2).Picture = LoadPicture("shz\im2.JPG")
Image1(3).Picture = LoadPicture("shz\im3.JPG")
Image1(4).Picture = LoadPicture("shz\im4.JPG")
Image1(5).Picture = LoadPicture("shz\im5.JPG")
Image1(6).Picture = LoadPicture("shz\im6.JPG")
Image1(7).Picture = LoadPicture("shz\im7.JPG")
Image1(8).Picture = LoadPicture("shz\im8.JPG")
Image1(9).Picture = LoadPicture("shz\im9.JPG")


Image1(1).Visible = True
Image1(2).Visible = False
Image1(3).Visible = False
Image1(4).Visible = False
Image1(5).Visible = False
Image1(6).Visible = False
Image1(7).Visible = False
Image1(8).Visible = False
Image1(9).Visible = False

counter = 1
End Sub
```

Project 14: An application to manage temporary memory data of Operating System (OS Clipboard Operations)

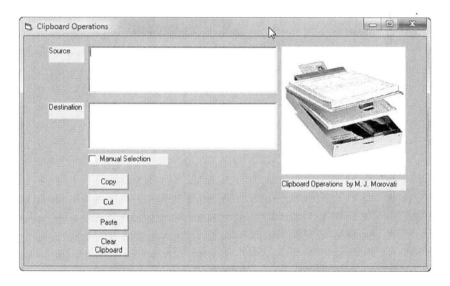

Educational goals of the project:

Understanding and using the functions of the operating system clipboard memory in Visual Basic

Summary of design, implementation, and execution of the project:

The application considers data written in the "Source" TextBox; copy data to the operating system clipboard with the "Copy" button (using

Clipboard.setText routine); cut data to the clipboard with the "cut" button, and paste data from the clipboard to "Destination" TextBox with the "paste" button (using Clipboard.getText routine). "Clipboard.selText" routine can be used to copy only selected data to the clipboard (checkbox must be checked).

Using "Clipboard.clear" routine, the clipboard data is deleted by pressing "Clear" button.

Development proposals:

Design a program that monitors data in the clipboard every 10 seconds, using the timer control.

The program has the ability to copy an image into the clipboard and get it from the clipboard.

Project source code:

```
Private Sub Command1_Click()
If (CheckSelect.Value = vbChecked) Then
   Clipboard.SetText (Text1.SelText)
Else
   Clipboard.SetText (Text1.Text)
End If

End Sub

Private Sub Command2_Click()
Text2.Text = Clipboard.GetText

End Sub

Private Sub Command3_Click()
If (CheckSelect.Value = vbChecked) Then
   Clipboard.SetText (Text1.SelText)
   Text1.SelText = ""
Else
   Clipboard.SetText (Text1.Text)
   Text1.Text = ""
End If
End Sub
```

```
Private Sub Command4_Click()
Clipboard.Clear
End Sub
```

Project 15: Ticket reservation application

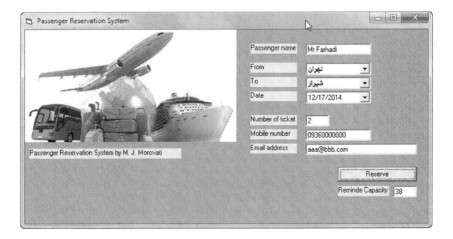

Educational goals of the project:

Understanding and using the ListBox and ComboBox controls in Visual Basic

Summary of design, implementation, and execution of the project:

Many parts of the reservation application can be implemented with the ComboBox control to select from different options, such as origin, destination, date of travel, and so on. These controls are initialized with the correct values in Form_load module. Additional fields for gathering information such as name, email, phone number, and the number of tickets are added to the form. When the operator fills the form fields, by pressing the "Reserve" button, a report about passenger ticket reservation is generated.

Default capacity of the vehicle is assumed to be 40. With any ticket reservation, capacity will be deducted according to the number of tickets ordered. Finally, with zero residual capacity, the Reserve button will be disabled.

Development proposals:

Add additional fields, such as seat number, food, and calculation of the cost of tickets according to the origin, destination, and food. The ticket is saved in a file. Apply Field validation of application fields.

Project source code:

```
Private Sub Command1_Click()

Dim message As String
Dim intconfirm As Integer

message = "Name : " & Text1 & vbNewLine & " From : " & Combo1.Text
& vbNewLine & " To : " & Combo2.Text & vbNewLine & " Date : " &
Combo3.Text & vbNewLine & "Num of Passenger : " & Text5.Text &
vbNewLine & " Mobile number : " & Text2 & vbNewLine & " Email
address : " & Text3 & "    Confirm ?"
intconfirm = MsgBox(message, vbYesNoCancel, "Confirm")

If (intconfirm = vbYes) Then
   If (Val(Text4) < Val(Text5)) Then
     MsgBox ("Not enough capacity")
   Else
     Text4 = Val(Text4) - Val(Text5)
     If (Val(Text4) = 0) Then
        Command1.Enabled = False
     End If
   End If
End If
End Sub

Private Sub Form_Load()
Text4.Text = 40
```

```
Combo1.List(0) = "Tehran"
Combo1.List(1) = "Tabriz"
Combo1.List(2) = "Shiraz"
Combo1.List(3) = "Yazd"

Combo2.List(0) = "Tehran"
Combo2.List(1) = "Tabriz"
Combo2.List(2) = "Shiraz"
Combo2.List(3) = "Yazd"

Combo3.List(0) = Date
Combo3.List(1) = Date + 1
Combo3.List(2) = Date + 2
Combo3.List(3) = Date + 3
Combo3.List(4) = Date + 4

End Sub
```

Project 16: Operation execution program with keyboard and mouse buttons

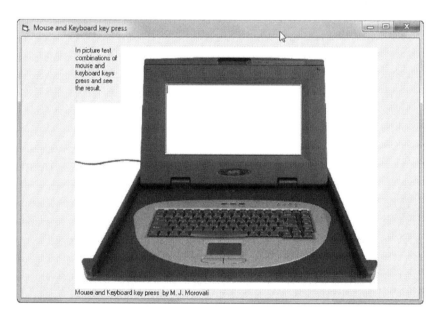

Educational goals of the project:

Understanding and using the mouse and keyboard events and functions and their arguments in Visual Basic

Understanding the concept of Shortcut key in programs

Summary of design, implementation, and execution of the project:

In "Mouse Down" routine of the application, combination of mouse button press, ALT, Shift, and Ctrl keyboard key press are checked with "Button" and "Shift" arguments of "Mouse Down" routine. The values are as follows:

"Button" value	Mouse Click
1	Left
2	Right
4	Scroll

"Shift" value	Keyboard keys
1	Shift
2	Ctrl
4	ALT
3	Ctrl+Shift
5	Alt+Shift
6	Alt+Ctrl
7	Alt+Ctrl+Shift

Development proposals:

For various combinations of mouse and keyboard buttons, design an operation in the operating system, as Shortcut key.

Project source code:

```
Private Sub Image1_MouseDown(Button As Integer, Shift As Integer, X As Single, Y As Single)
Text1.Text = ""

Select Case Shift
Case 1
   Text1.Text = "KeyBoard Shift key"
Case 2
   Text1.Text = "KeyBoard Ctrl key"
Case 3
   Text1.Text = "KeyBoard Ctrl + Shift key"
Case 4
   Text1.Text = "KeyBoard ALT key"
Case 5
   Text1.Text = "KeyBoard ALT + Shift key"
Case 6
```

```
    Text1.Text = "KeyBoard ALT + Ctrl key"
Case 7
    Text1.Text = "KeyBoard ALT + Ctrl + Shift key"
End Select

Select Case Button
Case 1
    Text1.Text = Text1.Text & vbNewLine & "Mouse Left Click"

Case 2
    Text1.Text = Text1.Text & vbNewLine & "Mouse Right Click"

Case 4
    Text1.Text = Text1.Text & vbNewLine & "Mouse Scroll Click"

End Select

End Sub
```

Project 17: A program to sort 100-meter-race record times

Educational goals of the project:

Understanding the definition and structure of arrays in Visual Basic

Understanding and using ListBox control in Visual Basic

Understanding random number generation in Visual Basic

Understanding and using the Bubble-Sort data sorting algorithm

Summary of design, implementation, and execution of the project:

By pressing the "Results" button in the application, ten random numbers between 8 and 18 are generated as time records of ten 100-meter race runners. Generated numbers are inserted in the List1 ListBox. Pressing the "Rank" button applies Bubble-Sort on list 1 in an ascending way, and the results are inserted in the List2 ListBox. The race results will be saved in a file. Research about the Bubble-Sort algorithm.

Development proposals:

Develop an application for managing a public running race (for example race with 5,000 runners) so that by the end of each runner's effort, his time record is registered in the runners' list, and the list remains sorted.

Project source code:

```
Option Base 1
Dim sngarrayA(10) As Single

Private Sub Command1_Click()
Dim i As Integer
List1.Clear

For i = LBound(sngarrayA) To UBound(sngarrayA)
    sngarrayA(i) = (Rnd * 10) + 8
    List1.AddItem sngarrayA(i)
Next

End Sub

Private Sub Command2_Click()
Dim intpass As Integer, intcomp As Integer
Dim temp As Single
Dim inti As Integer
List2.Clear

For intpass = LBound(sngarrayA) To UBound(sngarrayA) - 1
    For intcomp = LBound(sngarrayA) To UBound(sngarrayA) - intpass

        If sngarrayA(intcomp) > sngarrayA(intcomp + 1) Then
            temp = sngarrayA(intcomp)
            sngarrayA(intcomp) = sngarrayA(intcomp + 1)
            sngarrayA(intcomp + 1) = temp
        End If
    Next
Next
```

```
For inti = LBound(sngarrayA) To UBound(sngarrayA)
    List2.AddItem sngarrayA(inti)
Next

End Sub
```

Project 18: The computer terminology dictionary application implemented by Linear and Binary Search methods

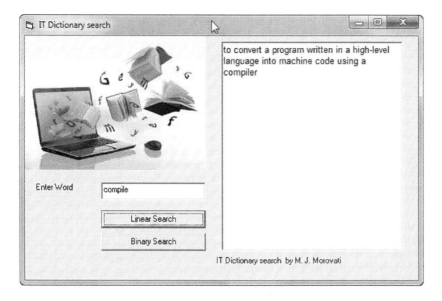

Educational goals of the project:

Understanding and using ListBox control in Visual Basic

Understanding and using Linear and Binary data search algorithms

Summary of design, implementation, and execution of the project:

In the following application, some English computer-related terms and their definitions are gathered in two lists (here, there are five terms: Debug,

Compile, Desktop, Hack, and Network, and their definitions initialized in Form_Load module). The user enters a term and selects either the binary search or linear search method to search the definition of the term.

Binary search is much faster than linear search in a sorted search list, so before performing a binary search algorithm, the sorting algorithm must be applied to the search list. Research about the two search algorithms and their structure and speed.

Development proposals:

Develop an application to perform searches on the search list in a text file. Collect audio pronunciation of words and phrases and play them in searches (the sound play in the program can be implemented by calling and using its API routines).

Project source code:

```
Private Sub Command2_Click()
Text2.Text = ""
Dim word As String
word = Text1.Text

Dim intLow As Integer
Dim intHigh As Integer
Dim intMid As Integer
intLow = 0
intHigh = 4

Do While (intLow <= intHigh)
    intMid = (intLow + intHigh) \ 2
    If word < (List1.List(intMid)) Then
        intHigh = intMid - 1
    ElseIf word > (List1.List(intMid)) Then
        intLow = intMid + 1
    Else
        Text2.Text = List2.List(intMid)
        Exit Do
    End If
Loop

End Sub
```

```vb
Private Sub Command3_Click()
Text2.Text = ""
Dim word As String
word = Text1.Text

Dim intL As Integer
Dim intH As Integer

intL = 0
intH = 4

Dim i As Integer
For i = intL To intH
   If (List1.List(i) = word) Then
      Text2.Text = List2.List(i)
      Exit For
   End If
Next

End Sub

Private Sub Form_Load()

List1.List(0) = "compile"
List1.List(1) = "debug"
List1.List(2) = "desktop"
List1.List(3) = "hack"
List1.List(4) = "network"

List2.List(0) = "to convert a program written in a high-level language into
machine code using a compiler"
List2.List(1) = "to find and fix errors or bugs in a program or system"
List2.List(2) = "the main graphical user interface background screen that
displays icons for other programs"
List2.List(3) = "to gain unauthorized access to a network system"
List2.List(4) = "a combination of a number of computers and peripheral
devices connected together"


End Sub
```

Project 19: The application of color composition and selection in RGB color systems (same as Adobe Photoshop color palette)

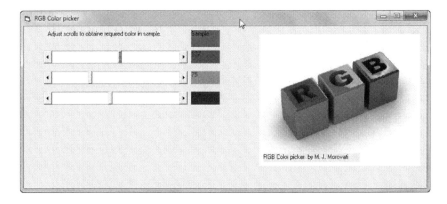

Educational goals of the project:

Understanding and using Scroll control in Visual Basic

Understanding and using the RGB color function to define RGB color in Visual Basic

Summary of design, implementation, and execution of the project:

In the following application, three Scroll controls in the range of 0-256, as red, green, and blue color ranges, are embedded.

In any changes in the scrolls, new values are passed to RGB function, and composed color is applied to the "Sample" label.

Development proposals:

Develop an application to compose colors in other color systems, such as CMYK

Project source code:

```
Dim r As Integer
Dim g As Integer
Dim b As Integer

Private Sub Form_Load()
Label4.BackColor = RGB(0, 0, 0)

Label1.BackColor = vbRed
Label2.BackColor = vbGreen
Label3.BackColor = vbBlue

End Sub

Private Sub HScroll1_Change()

r = HScroll1.Value
g = HScroll2.Value
b = HScroll3.Value

Label1.Caption = r
Label2.Caption = g
Label3.Caption = b

Label4.BackColor = RGB(r, g, b)

End Sub

Private Sub HScroll2_Change()

r = HScroll1.Value
g = HScroll2.Value
b = HScroll3.Value
```

```
Label1.Caption = r
Label2.Caption = g
Label3.Caption = b

Label4.BackColor = RGB(r, g, b)

End Sub

Private Sub HScroll3_Change()

r = HScroll1.Value
g = HScroll2.Value
b = HScroll3.Value

Label1.Caption = r
Label2.Caption = g
Label3.Caption = b

Label4.BackColor = RGB(r, g, b)

End Sub
```

Project 20: The File Management application

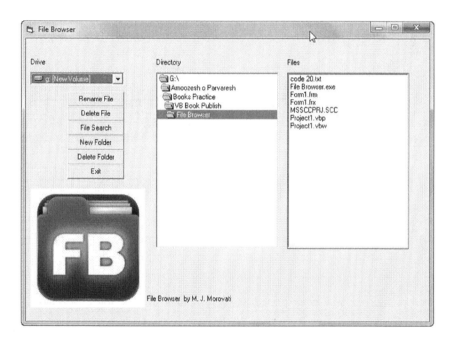

Educational goals of the project:

Understanding and using DirListBox, FileListBox, and DriveListBox controls in Visual Basic

Understanding and using functions and commands to manage files and directories in Visual Basic

Summary of design, implementation, and execution of the project:

When the project runs, the default path will be the directory containing the current project files. The program includes drive select control (DriveListBox), directory selection control (DirListBox), and file selection control (FileListBox). These controls are linked together using the following code to provide a browseable path.

In Drive control:
$$Dir1.Path = Drive1.Drive$$
In Directory control:
$$File1.Path = Dir1.Path$$

Now, system file management functions, such as changing the file name (Name), deleting files (Kill), searching for files (Dir), creating a new folder (MkDir), and removing the folder (RmDir) are implemented and provided for the user.

Development proposals:

Implement this project with FSO (file system object) functions and procedures, instead of the above solution, and develop system file management commands in the application. Add a Preview option to the application for image and text files.

Project source code:

```
Dim StrFilePath As String
Dim StrDirPath As String


Private Sub Command1_Click()
Dim StrNewName As String
Dim StrNewPath As String

StrNewName = InputBox("Enter new FileName", "Rename")

StrNewPath = File1.Path
If Right(File1.Path, 1) <> "\" Then
    StrNewPath = StrNewPath + "\"
End If
Name StrFilePath As StrNewPath + StrNewName
```

```
End Sub

Private Sub Command2_Click()
Dim intA As Integer
intA = MsgBox("Permanently Delete the file " + StrFilePath + " ?",
vbYesNo, "Deletion")
If intA = vbYes Then Kill StrFilePath

End Sub

Private Sub Command3_Click()
Dim StrSearch As String
StrSearch = Trim(InputBox("Enter FileName to search", "Search"))
If Dir(StrSearch) <> "" Then
    MsgBox ("File Found.")
Else
    MsgBox ("File not Found.")
End If

End Sub

Private Sub Command4_Click()
Dim StrDirName As String
StrDirName = Trim(InputBox("Enter NewFolder name", "NewFolder"))
MkDir StrDirPath + StrDirName

End Sub

Private Sub Command5_Click()
Dim DeletePath As String
Dim intA As Integer

DeletePath = StrDirPath

intA = MsgBox("Permanently Delete the Folder " + DeletePath + " ?",
vbYesNo, "Deletion")
If intA = vbYes Then
    ChDir ".."
    RmDir DeletePath
End If

End Sub
```

```
Private Sub Command6_Click()
End
End Sub

Private Sub Dir1_Change()
ChDir Dir1.Path
File1.Path = Dir1.Path

StrDirPath = Dir1.Path
Label1.Caption = StrDirPath

End Sub

Private Sub Drive1_Change()
ChDrive Drive1.Drive
Dir1.Path = Drive1.Drive

End Sub

Private Sub File1_Click()
StrFilePath = File1.Path

If Right(File1.Path, 1) <> "\" Then
   StrFilePath = StrFilePath + "\"
End If
StrFilePath = StrFilePath + File1.List(File1.ListIndex)

Label2.Caption = StrFilePath
End Sub
```

Project 21: A program to solve and implement sample problem using object-oriented programming method

Educational goals of the project:

Understanding the concepts of object-oriented programming and implementing it in Visual Basic

Learning how to define properties, methods, and classes for object-oriented programming in Visual Basic

Summary of design, implementation, and execution of the project:

The application calculates the area of a rectangle with object-oriented programming. The program consists of a rectangle object (Class 1), which has a length property (length) and width property (width); functions for calculating perimeter and area in a rectangle. In the main program, an instance of rectangle class is created (rec1), and the length and width properties are initialized with values that the user enters. The functions are performed and the result is printed.

Development proposals:

In a more complex project, design an object-oriented programming model and implement objects, properties, and functions of the project.

Project source code:

```
Class1
Dim m_length As Integer, m_width As Integer
Public Property Get length() As Variant
 length = m_length
End Property

Public Property Let length(ByVal vNewValue As Variant)
m_length = vNewValue
End Property

Public Property Get width() As Variant
 width = m_width
End Property

Public Property Let width(ByVal vNewValue As Variant)
m_width = vNewValue
End Property

Public Function primeter() As Integer
  primeter = (m_length + m_width) * 2
  End Function


Public Function area() As Integer
area = m_length * m_width
End Function


Form 1
```

```
Private Sub Command1_Click()

Dim rec1 As New Class1
rec1.width = InputBox("Enter width of rectangle:")
rec1.length = InputBox("Enter length of rectangle:")
Print "Primeter :" & rec1.primeter
Print "Area :" & rec1.area

End Sub
```

Project 22: Text Editor

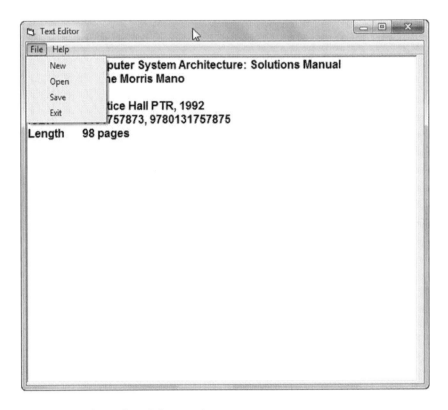

Educational goals of the project:

Understanding the structure of a Text Editor program

Understanding and using the Common Dialog control to create common dialog boxes, such as opening files, saving files, printing files, and setting the font and color of the text files

Understanding menu design tool in Visual Basic (Menu Editor Tool)

Understanding and using the functions of reading and writing data in files (File Operations) in Visual Basic

Understanding the Call statement in Visual Basic

Summary of design, implementation, and execution of the project:

The application includes a text box to the size of the application window, with an activated Multiline property, and the menus are designed with the Menu Editor Tool. In the "Save" submenu, the content of the text box is written into a file, and in the "Open" submenu, the text file content is loaded into the Text Editor TextBox.

Code to write data into a text file:

```
Open strFilename For Output As #intFile
Print #intFile, strText
Close #intFile
```

Code to read line-by-line data from a text file line-by-line:

```
Open strFilename For Input As #intFile
Do While Not EOF (intFile)
        Line Input #intFile, strBuffer
        strText = strText & strBuffer & vbCrLf
    Loop
Close #intFile
```

"Close #intFile" used at the end to close the file.

In the sub-menus, saving and opening dialogs are implemented with the Common Dialog control (cdMain.ShowSave for saving in a file, and cdMain.ShowOpen for opening file).

Note: To use the Common Dialog control, first you should add the "Microsoft Common Dialog Control 6.0" Component to the toolbox, in the Project menu.

Development proposals:

Add some other submenus to the text editor application to make it similar to the Notepad application in Windows, such as setting the font, setting the color and text display, and print operation (all of these are implemented using the Command Dialog control commands like cdMain.ShowFont, cdMain.ShowColor, and cdMain.ShowPrinter).

Add "Find and Replace" ability to the application.

Include Shortcut keys to menus and submenus.

Project source code:

```
Dim strFilter As String

Private Sub exitmenu_Click()
Dim intA As Integer

intA = MsgBox("Do you want to Save Document?", vbYesNoCancel, Save)
If (intA = vbNo) Then
    End
ElseIf (intA = vbYes) Then
    Call savemenu_Click
End If

End Sub

Private Sub helpmenu_Click()
MsgBox ("Text Editor v1.0")
End Sub

Private Sub newmenu_Click()
Dim intA As Integer

intA = MsgBox("Do you want to Save Document?", vbYesNoCancel, Save)

If (intA = vbYes) Then
    Call savemenu_Click
End If
Text1.Text = ""
End Sub

Private Sub openmenu_Click()

Dim strFilename As String
Dim strText As String
```

```
Dim strBuffer As String
Dim intFile As Integer

strFilter = "text(*.text)|*.text|All Files(*.*)|*.*"
cdMain.ShowOpen
If (cdMain.FileName <> "") Then
   strFilename = cdMain.FileName
   intFile = FreeFile

   Open strFilename For Input As #intFile

   MousePointer = vbHourglass

   Do While Not EOF(intFile)
      Line Input #intFile, strBuffer
      strText = strText & strBuffer & vbCrLf

   Loop

   MousePointer = vbDefault
   Close #intFile

   Text1.Text = strText
End If

End Sub

Private Sub savemenu_Click()

Dim strFilename As String
Dim strText As String
Dim intFile As Integer

strFilter = "text(*.textt)|*.text|All Filess(*.*)|*.*"
cdMain.Filter = strFilter
cdMain.ShowSave
If (cdMain.FileName <> "") Then
   strFilename = cdMain.FileName
   strText = Text1.Text
   intFile = FreeFile

   Open strFilename For Output As #intFile
```

```
    MousePointer = vbHourglass
    Print #intFile, strText
    MousePointer = vbDefault

    Close #intFile
End If


End Sub
```

Project 23: Microsoft Word text file grammar and spell checker application

Educational goals of the project:

Understanding how the Visual basic application and Microsoft Office software are linked to each other

Understanding and using the Word object properties and methods for working with Microsoft Word text files

Summary of design, implementation, and execution of the project:

Visual Basic software has the ability to use ActiveX components of library files (olb) from software installed on the system. In this project, the library file of the "Microsoft Word 14.0 Object library" is selected from the References option in Project menu.

In this application, the desired text file called Test.docx, is placed in the D:\ drive. By pressing the "Check Spell" button:

An instance of the Word.Application object is created, and the "Test.docx" file is opened. (wd.Documents.Open)

"MyRange" range is defined, and includes the entire text file (Set myRange = wd.ActiveDocument.Content)

The "SpellingChecked" method analyzes grammar and spelling correctness of "myrange" range, print grammar, and spelling correctness in TextBox.

In the end, the file should be closed (wd.Quit and wd.Documents.Close), and the content of the object should be deleted (Set wd = Nothing).

Development proposals:

Use the Common Dialog control in the application to choose the file from the file browser for grammar spell checking.

Practice with Library files from other software installed on the system.

Project source code:

```
Private Sub Command1_Click()

Dim wd As New Word.Application
Dim myRange As Word.Range
Dim SpellChecked As Boolean

wd.Documents.Open ("D:\Test.docx")
Set myRange = wd.ActiveDocument.Content

SpellChecked = myRange.SpellingChecked

If SpellChecked = True Then
   Text1.Text = "Spell checked OK."
Else
   Text1.Text = "Spell checked Error."
End If

wd.Documents.Close
wd.Quit
Set wd = Nothing

End Sub
```

Project 24: The application for opening and closing the CD-Drive and DVD-Drive

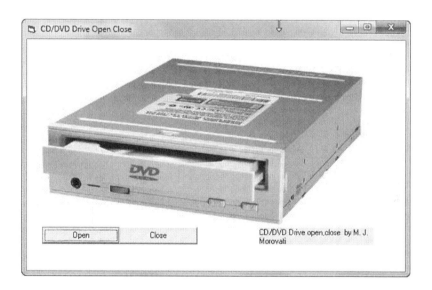

Educational goals of the project:

Understanding and using Windows API routines stored in DLL files

Understanding the API Viewer utility to view and call API routines with the Declare statement in Visual Basic

Summary of design, implementation, and execution of the project:

API viewer tool is available through the Visual Basic installation path in the "Microsoft visual basic 6.0 tools" section in the start menu. Many of the common API routines are located in the "WIN32API.txt" file. This file is loaded using "Load Text File" option in "File" menu of the API Viewer tool. The Declare option is selected in the API list type, and the "mciSendString" routine code is copied in the project.

By pressing the "Open" and "Close" buttons, "mciSendString" routines will run with its arguments related to the opening and closing operations of the CD/DVD Drive.

Development proposals:

Schedule opening and closing operations of CD/DVD Drive.

Try other applicable API routines; for example, playing audio files (SndPlaySound () routine), taking pictures of the screen (PaintDesktop () routine), a beep by the sound card (messagebeep () routine), etc...

Project source code:

```
Private Declare Function mciSendString Lib "winmm.dll" Alias
"mciSendStringA" (ByVal lpstrCommand As String, ByVal
lpstrReturnString As String, ByVal uReturnLength As Long, ByVal
hwndCallback As Long) As Long


Private Sub Command1_Click()
mciSendString "set CDAudio Door Open wait", 0&, 0&, 0&
End Sub


Private Sub Command2_Click()
mciSendString "set CDAudio Door Closed wait", 0&, 0&, 0&
End Sub
```

Project 25: The multimedia player

Educational goals of the project:

Understanding the structure of a Multimedia Player application

Understanding and using "MultiMedia Control" component to play audio and video files

Understanding and applying properties and procedures of the

"MultiMedia Control" component, such as Play, Pause, Stop, Next, Seek, etc.

Summary of design, implementation, and execution of the project:

To select a file from the file system, use the "Common Dialog" control, and to play audio and video files, use the "MultiMedia Control" component. Thus, these controls are added to the project.

The "MultiMedia Control" component has some important properties:

1." FileName" is used for playing a file with a specified path

2. "DeviceType" is used to play audio file with ".Wav" extension, should have a value of "Wav Audio", and to play video file with an ".Avi" extension, it should have a value of "AviVideo". Choosing audio or video files is done with an object button in the form. To play a video file, a PictureBox control should be placed on the application form. To link the PictureBox and MultiMedia Controls to play a video file, the following code is used:

$$MMControl1.hWndDisplay = Picture1.hWnd$$

3. "Command": commands related to playing audio and video files, such as Open, Play, Pause, Stop, Next, Seek, etc; pass to this property.

Development proposals:

Try other MultiMedia Control commands. For example, by embedding the possibility to select multiple files for automatic play, Command Next, Previous, and more.

Check how to play other audio and video file formats (more than Wav and Avi).

Add common features in multimedia player applications, such as display a list of files and their properties, elapsed time of each track, volume control, voice recording with microphone, etc....

Project source code:

```
Private Sub CommandOpen_Click()

If OptionWav.Value = True Then
    MMControl1.DeviceType = "WaveAudio"

ElseIf OptionAvi.Value = True Then
```

```
      MMControl1.DeviceType = "AviVideo"
      MMControl1.hWndDisplay = Picture1.hWnd
End If

CommonDialog1.Filter = "*.*"
CommonDialog1.ShowOpen

If CommonDialog1.FileName <> "" Then
      MMControl1.FileName = CommonDialog1.FileName
      MMControl1.Command = "Open"
      MMControl1.Command = "Play"
      CommandPlay.Caption = "Pause"
End If

End Sub

Private Sub CommandPlay_Click()

If CommandPlay.Caption = "Pause" Then
      CommandPlay.Caption = "Play"
      MMControl1.Command = "Pause"

ElseIf CommandPlay.Caption = "Play" Then
      CommandPlay.Caption = "Pause"
      MMControl1.Command = "Play"
End If

End Sub

Private Sub CommandStop_Click()

MMControl1.Command = "Stop"

End Sub

Private Sub Form_Load()

OptionWav.Value = True

End Sub
```

Project 26: The management application of running processes in the operating system

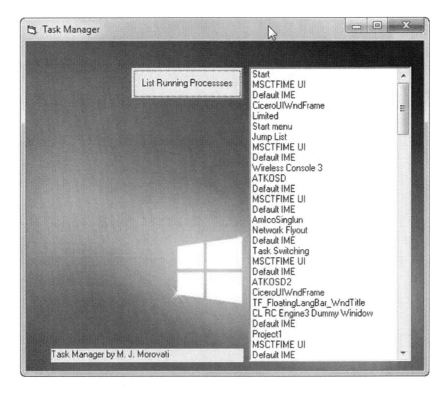

Educational goals of the project:

Understanding the process management concept in operating systems

Understanding and using the Windows API routines stored in DLL files

Understanding the API Viewer utility to view and call API routines with the Declare statement in Visual Basic

Understanding the process management functions in Visual Basic

Summary of design, implementation, and execution of the project:

API routines needed to get the operating system running processes' information are introduced. Then using "GetWindow" and "GetWindowText" functions, the required information is received, and a list of running processes is displayed in the ListBox.

Development proposals:

Add new options to the application, such as display processes information, terminate processes (End Process), start processes, and pause running processes.

Implement running processes management with the "process" class and its properties and methods, instead of using API routines.

Project source code:

```
Private Declare Function GetWindow Lib "user32" (ByVal hwnd As Long,
ByVal wCmd As Long) As Long
Private Declare Function GetParent Lib "user32" (ByVal hwnd As Long)
As Long
Private Declare Function GetWindowTextLength Lib "user32" Alias
"GetWindowTextLengthA" (ByVal hwnd As Long) As Long
Private Declare Function GetWindowText Lib "user32" Alias
"GetWindowTextA" (ByVal hwnd As Long, ByVal lpString As String,
ByVal cch As Long) As Long
Private Declare Function FindWindow Lib "user32" Alias "FindWindowA"
(ByVal lpClassName As String, ByVal lpWindowName As String) As Long
Private Declare Function CloseWindow Lib "user32" (ByVal hwnd As
Long) As Long

Const GW_HWNDFIRST = 0
Const GW_HWNDNEXT = 2
Dim handel

Private Sub Command1_Click()
```

```
    Dim CurrWnd As Long
    Dim Length As Long
    Dim TaskName As String
    List1.Clear
    CurrWnd = GetWindow(Form1.hwnd, GW_HWNDFIRST)
    While CurrWnd <> 0

        Length = GetWindowTextLength(CurrWnd)
        TaskName = Space$(Length + 1)
        Length = GetWindowText(CurrWnd, TaskName, Length + 1)
        TaskName = Left$(TaskName, Len(TaskName) - 1)

        If Length > 0 Then
           If TaskName <> Me.Caption Then
              List1.AddItem TaskName
           End If
        End If
        CurrWnd = GetWindow(CurrWnd, GW_HWNDNEXT)
        DoEvents
    Wend
End Sub
Private Sub Form_Load()

End Sub
```

Appendix 1: Visual Basic Commands References

Declarations

☐   Dim - Used to define a variable as a certain type. DIM is the simplest way to declare a variable.

Dim *varName* as *VarType*

     Possible types include **Integer, String, Double** (floating point), Boolean

VB will let you leave off the *VarType* declaration, or let you use **Object** (the equivalent was called *Variant* in VB6) as the type (can store any type). Both of these options are **<u>bad</u>** ideas: then YOU have to keep track of the type of the variable and make sure you do the right thing. Use types, so that VB can help you find your bugs.

☐   Const - Creates a variable whose value is fixed

Const kgToPound = 2.205

☐   Call - Transfers control to a Sub or Function (is optional)

Call Procedure 1

Since the use of CALL is optional, you can ignore this.

☐   Sub - Defines a method which can execute a block of code

Sub *methodName* (var1 as *VarType*, var2 as *VarType*, var3 as *VarType*)
Be sure to check out HELP for how to handle Sub's arguments.

☐   Function - Declares a procedure which can return a value
Function *functionName* (var1 as *VarType*, var2 as *VarType*) as *VarType*

This is the most versatile of the Sub/Function procedure types. It can do anything a Sub can do as well as returning a value for use in an expression.

To return a value:
functionName = value

Operators

/ - Normal division
\ - Integer division (truncates the answer)
^ - Exponentiation operator
* - Multiply
+ - Plus
- - Minus
= - Equal
> - Greater Than
< - Less Than
<> - Not Equal
>= - Greater than or equal
<= - Less than or equal
AND - Defines a boolean value that is the AND of two values
result = expression1 AND expression2
OR - Defines a boolean value that is the OR of two values
result = expression1 OR expression2
IS - Determines if 2 variables reference the same object
result = object1 IS object2
LIKE - Determines if one string matches a pattern
result = string LIKE pattern

Math Functions

.NET Framework method	Description
Abs	Returns the absolute value of a number.
Acos	Returns the angle whose cosine is the specified number.
Asin	Returns the angle whose sine is the specified number.
Atan	Returns the angle whose tangent is the specified number.
Atan2	Returns the angle whose tangent is the quotient of two specified numbers.
BigMul	Returns the full product of two 32-bit numbers.
Ceiling	Returns the smallest integral value that's greater than or equal to the specified **Decimal** or **Double**.
Cos	Returns the cosine of the specified angle.

Cosh	Returns the hyperbolic cosine of the specified angle.
DivRem	Returns the quotient of two 32-bit or 64-bit signed integers, and also returns the remainder in an output parameter.
Exp	Returns e (the base of natural logarithms) raised to the specified power.
Floor	Returns the largest integer that's less than or equal to the specified **Decimal** or **Double** number.
IEEERemain der	Returns the remainder that results from the division of a specified number by another specified number.
Log	Returns the natural (base e) logarithm of a specified number or the logarithm of a specified number in a specified base.
Log10	Returns the base 10 logarithm of a specified number.
Max	Returns the larger of two numbers.
Min	Returns the smaller of two numbers.

Pow	Returns a specified number raised to the specified power.
Round	Returns a **Decimal** or **Double** value rounded to the nearest integral value or to a specified number of fractional digits.
Sign	Returns an **Integer** value indicating the sign of a number.
Sin	Returns the sine of the specified angle.
Sinh	Returns the hyperbolic sine of the specified angle.
Sqrt	Returns the square root of a specified number.
Tan	Returns the tangent of the specified angle.
Tanh	Returns the hyperbolic tangent of the specified angle.
Truncate	Calculates the integral part of a specified **Decimal** or **Double** number.

Type Conversions

Function name	Return data type	Range for *expression* argument
CBool	Boolean Data Type (Visual Basic)	Any valid **Char** or **String** or numeric expression.
CByte	Byte Data Type (Visual Basic)	0 through 255 (unsigned); fractional parts are rounded.
CChar	Char Data Type (Visual Basic)	Any valid **Char** or **String** expression; only first character of a **String** is converted; value can be 0 through 65535 (unsigned).
CDate	Date Data Type (Visual Basic)	Any valid representation of a date and time.
CDbl	Double Data Type (Visual Basic)	-1.79769313486231570E+308 through -4.94065645841246544E-324 for negative values; 4.94065645841246544E-324 through 1.79769313486231570E+308 for positive values.

CDec	Decimal Data Type (Visual Basic)	+/- 79,228,162,514,264,337,593,543,950,335 for zero-scaled numbers, that is, numbers with no decimal places. For numbers with 28 decimal places, the range is +/- 7.9228162514264337593543950335. The smallest possible non-zero number is 0.0000000000000000000000000001 (+/-1E-28).
CInt	Integer Data Type (Visual Basic)	-2,147,483,648 through 2,147,483,647; fractional parts are rounded.
CLng	Long Data Type (Visual Basic)	-9,223,372,036,854,775,808 through 9,223,372,036,854,775,807; fractional parts are rounded.
CObj	Object Data Type	Any valid expression.
CSByte	SByte Data Type (Visual Basic)	-128 through 127; fractional parts are rounded.
CShort	Short Data Type (Visual Basic)	-32,768 through 32,767; fractional parts are rounded.

CSng	Single Data Type (Visual Basic)	-3.402823E+38 through -1.401298E-45 for negative values; 1.401298E-45 through 3.402823E+38 for positive values.
CStr	String Data Type (Visual Basic)	Returns for **CStr** depend on the *expression* argument. See Return Values for the CStr Function (Visual Basic).
CUInt	UInteger Data Type	0 through 4,294,967,295 (unsigned); fractional parts are rounded.
CULng	ULong Data Type (Visual Basic)	0 through 18,446,744,073,709,551,615 (unsigned); fractional parts are rounded.
CUShort	UShort Data Type (Visual Basic)	0 through 65,535 (unsigned); fractional parts are rounded.

Strings Functions

.NET Framework method	Description
Asc , AscW	Returns an **Integer** value representing the character code corresponding to a character.
Chr , ChrW	Returns the character associated with the specified character code.
Filter	Returns a zero-based array containing a subset of a **String** array based on specified filter criteria.
Format	Returns a string formatted according to instructions contained in a format **String** expression.

FormatCurrency	Returns an expression formatted as a currency value using the currency symbol defined in the system control panel.
FormatDateTime	Returns a string expression representing a date/time value.
FormatNumber	Returns an expression formatted as a number.
FormatPercent	Returns an expression formatted as a percentage (that is, multiplied by 100) with a trailing % character.
InStr	Returns an integer specifying the start position of the first occurrence of one string within another.
InStrRev	Returns the position of the first occurrence of one string within another, starting from the right side of the string.

Join	Returns a string created by joining a number of substrings contained in an array.
LCase	Returns a string or character converted to lowercase.
Left	Returns a string containing a specified number of characters from the left side of a string.
Len	Returns an integer that contains the number of characters in a string.
LSet	Returns a left-aligned string containing the specified string adjusted to the specified length.
LTrim	Returns a string containing a copy of a specified string with no leading spaces.
Mid	Returns a string containing a specified number of characters from a string.

Replace	Returns a string in which a specified substring has been replaced with another substring a specified number of times.
Right	Returns a string containing a specified number of characters from the right side of a string.
RSet	Returns a right-aligned string containing the specified string adjusted to the specified length.
RTrim	Returns a string containing a copy of a specified string with no trailing spaces.
Space	Returns a string consisting of the specified number of spaces.
Split	Returns a zero-based, one-dimensional array containing a specified number of substrings.
StrComp	Returns -1, 0, or 1, based on the result of a string comparison.

StrConv	Returns a string converted as specified.
StrDup	Returns a string or object consisting of the specified character repeated the specified number of times.
StrReverse	Returns a string in which the character order of a specified string is reversed.
Trim	Returns a string containing a copy of a specified string with no leading or trailing spaces.
UCase	Returns a string or character containing the specified string converted to uppercase.

Misc Functions

MsgBox - A built-in dialog box that gives a message and allows user input

x = msgbox "Read this!", vbokonly, "Test Message"

The result of which button the user clicked is saved in x.

InputBox - A built-in dialog box that allows entry of a text string

inputbox "Input a value!", 5

RGB - Returns a color value by inputting the red, green, and blue parts

form1.backcolor = RGB (12,128,256)

Me - Refers to the current object, usually the active form

print Me.caption

Loops and Conditional Decisions

If..Then..Else - Performs code based on the results of a test

If A>5 Then Print "A is a bit number!"

For...Next - Loops a specified number of times

For i = 1 to 5: print #1, i: next i

For Each ... Next - Walks through a collection

For Each X in Form1.controls: Next X

While...Wend - Loops until an event is false

while i < 5: i = i +1: wend

Select Case - Takes an action based on a value of a parameter

select case i

case 1 : print "it was a 1"

case 2 : print "it was a 2"

end select

Do...Loop - Loops until conditions are met

```
do while i < 5 : i = i + 1 : loop
```

Choose - Selects and returns a value from a list of arguments

```
Choose (index, "answer1", "answer2", "answer3")
```

With - Executes a series of statements on a single object

```
With TextBox1

        .Height = 100

        .Width = 500

End With
```

End - Immediately stops execution of a program

```
End
```

Stop - Pauses execution of a program (can restart without loss of data)

```
Stop
```

References

1- برنامه سازی 1، علیرضا جباریه، کامبیز جمعدار، چاپ چهارم، 1390، انتشارات فاطمی

2- برنامه سازی 2، علیرضا جباریه، چاپ هفتم، 1391، انتشارات شرکت چاپ و نشر کتاب های درسی ایران

3- برنامه سازی 3، علیرضا جباریه، چاپ هفتم، 1391، انتشارات شرکت چاپ و نشر کتاب های درسی ایران

4- Visual Basic 6 How To Program, Harvey M. Deitel, Paul J. Deitel, Tem R. Nieto, 1999, Prentice Hall

5- Microsoft Visual Basic 6.0: Programmer's Guide, Microsoft Corporation, 1998, Microsoft Press

6- www.cs.cmu.edu

7- www.msdn.microsoft.com

ABOUT THE AUTHOR

Mohammad J. Morovati

Bachelor's degree, Computer Engineering, Shiraz University
High school Teacher of Computer science and programming
Fars province education organization
Shiraz, Iran

Printed in Great Britain
by Amazon